How to ⓒ
Write an Essay

Easy ways to write an essay.
Especially for students using
English as a second language

by
Phil Rashid BA Dip.Eur.Hum

authorHOUSE®

AuthorHouse™
1663 Liberty Drive
Bloomington, IN 47403
www.authorhouse.com
Phone: 1-800-839-8640

Published by AuthorHouse   06/22/2012

ISBN: 978-1-4685-8583-4 (sc)
ISBN: 978-1-4685-8585-8 (e)

Forward

Learning English as a second language can be daunting for beginners. I want to allay the fears that confront students. This book will show students that by applying the recommended methods, from the initial first written title to the final concluding paragraph, they will find a clear way of essay construction.

I hope they will enjoy future essay writing after mastering the techniques learnt from these instructions.

HAPPY WRITING

Phil Rashid

I dedicate this book to
my son Daniel
and
my daughter Aishah.

I thank them both
for giving me
the inspiration
needed to write it.

May they and others
benefit from
the knowledge
it may
give them.

Connectives: Words and Phrases

Addition

And
Also
furthermore
in addition
Too
again
the following
and then
what is more

moreover
as well as

Announcing/opinion

It would seem

one might consider/
suggest/propose/
image/ deduce/infer
to conclude

Summary

in brief
on the whole
throughout
in all
overall

to sum up
in summary

Illustration

for example
for instance
such as
as
as revealed by
thus
to show that
to take the case of

Cause & effect

consequently
thus
so
hence
as a result
because/as
therefore
accordingly
since

until
whenever
as long as

Emphasis

above all
in particular
notably
specifically
especially
significantly

more importantly
indeed
in fact

Sequence /Time

initially
first(ly)
then

so far

after (wards)
at last
finally
once
secondly
next
subsequently
meanwhile
at length

in the end
eventually

Comparison

equally
similarly
compared
an equivalent
in the same way
likewise
as with

Contrast/balance

but
however
nevertheless
alternatively

to turn to

yet
despite this
on the contrary
as for
the opposite
still

instead
on the other hand
whereas
otherwise
although

apart from

Persuasion (*Assuming the reader agrees*)

of course
naturally
obviously
clearly
evidently
surely
certainly

Restriction

only (if)
unless
except (for)
save for

SYMBOL	ERROR	CORRECTION
1. **SVA** SINGULAR - PLURAL	He **hath** been here for six **month.**	He **has** been here for six **months.**
2. **WF** WORD FORM	I saw a **beauty** picture.	I saw a **beautiful** picture.
3. **WC** WORD CHOICE	She got **on** the taxi.	She got **into** the taxi.
4. **VT** VERB TENSE	He **is** since June.	He **has been** since June.
5. **^** ADD A WORD	I want **^** go to the zoo.	I want **to** go to the zoo.
6. _ OMIT A WORD	She entered <u>**to**</u> the university.	She entered the university.
7. **WO** WORD ORDER	I saw **five times that movie.**	I saw **that movie five times.**
8. **INC.** INCOMPLETE	**Because I was tired.**	**I went to bed**, because I was tired.
9. **SP** SPELLING	An accident **hapened.**	An accident **happened.**
10. **P** PUNCTUATION	What did he say	What did he say**?**
11. **C** CAPITALISATION	I am an **e**nglishman.	I am an **E**nglishman.
12. **@** ARTICLE	I had **a** accident.	I had **an** accident.
13. **?** UNCLEAR MEANING	He borrowed a **writing thing.**	He borrowed a **pen.**
14. **RP** REPHRASE	Playing football **can exercise body.**	Playing football **is a good way to exercise the body.**

CONTENTS

Chapter One

Titles

Capital

Letters

and

Punctuation!

Capitalisation Rules

Rule 1. Capitalise the first word of a quoted sentence.

      Examples: *He said, "Treat her as you would your own daughter".*

      "Look out!" she screamed. "You almost ran into my child."

Rule 2. Capitalise a person's title, when it precedes the name. Don't capitalise when the title is acting as a description following the name. Examples: *Chairperson Petrov*

      Ms. Petrov, the chairperson of the company, is here.

Rule 3. Capitalise a proper noun..

      Example: *Tower Bridge.*

Rule 4. Capitalise when the person's title follows the name on the address or signature line.

      Examples: *Sincerely*   *Ms. Haines, Chairperson*

Rule 5. Capitalise the titles of high-ranking government officials when used with or before their names. Do not capitalise the civil title if it is used instead of the name.

      Examples: *The prime minister will address Parliament.*

      All members of parliament are expected to attend.

      The governors and lieutenant governors called for a special task force. Governor Jones, Lieutenant Governor Fairbanks, Attorney General Galloway and MP's James and Twain will attend.

Rule 6. Capitalise any title when used as a first address.

      Examples: *"Will you take my temperature, Doctor?"*

Rule 7. Capitalise points of a compass, only when they refer to specific regions.

      Examples: *We have had three relatives visit from the South.*

      Go South, three blocks and then turn left.

      We live in the <u>southeast</u> region of the town.

      <u>South east</u> is just an adjective here, describing a section so it should not be capitalised.

Rule 8. Capitalise Always capitalise the first and last words of publication titles regardless of their parts of speech. Always capitalise other words within titles, including the short verb forms **Is**, **Are** and **Be**. Don't capitalise words within titles such as, a, an, the , but, as, if, and, or, nor, or prepositions, regardless of their length

      Examples: *The Day of the Jackal*

      A Tale of Two Cities

      What Colour Is Your Parachute?

Capitalisation Rules

Rule 9.   **Capitalise**   *federal* or *state* when used as part of an official agency name
or in government documents where these terms represent
an official name. If they are being used as general terms,
lower-case letters may be used.
Examples: *The state has evidence to the contrary.*
That is a federal offence.
The State Board of Equalisation collects sales taxes.
We will visit three states during our summer vacation.
*The Federal Bureau of Investigation has been subject to much
scrutiny and criticism lately.*

Rule 10.   **Capitalise**   words such as department, bureau and office if you have
prepared your text in the following way.
Examples: The **B**ureau of **L**and **M**anagement (**B**ureau)
has some jurisdiction over **I**ndian lands. The **B**ureau is finding
its administrative role to be challenging.

Rule 11.   **Capitalise**   names of seasons, is wrong.
Example: *I love autumn colours.*
The first day of spring is almost here.

Rule 12.   **Capitalise**   the first word of a salutation and the first word of a
complimentary close.
Examples: **D**ear **M**s **M**ohammed:
My dear **M**r Sanchez:
Very truly yours.

Rule 13.   **Capitalise**   words derived from proper nouns.

Examples: *I must take English and maths. English*
is capitalised, because it comes from the proper noun, *England*,
but *maths* does not come from *mathland.*

Rule 14.   **Capitalise**   the names of specific course titles.
Example: *I must take history and Algebra 2.*

Titles

- Titles must be written to be able to be stood out and be noticed.

- They are always put together by other words.

- Words that are conjunction words and prepositions must ALWAYS be written in lower – case, (small letters).

Conjunctions	**Prepositions**	**Articles**
and; or; but; so	on; in; with; behind above; below; over under; for, of	a, an, the

- The exception is when they are at the beginning of a sentence or *title.*

- *Titles* must always be complete, (you may lose or not get any marks for incomplete *titles*).

- *Titles* must ALWAYS be <u>underlined</u>, or written in **bold** so that they are noticed.

An example:-
how to write an essay
<u>How to Write an Essay</u>

i)   two flew over the land of gold

_____

ii)   the sea and the wind

_____

iii)   the queen and I

_____

iv)   the magic of the mermaid

_____

v)   when the moment of my heart had gone

_____

CAPITAL *LETTERS* / *Prepositions*

Aa Bb Cc Dd **Ee** Ff Gg Hh **Ii** Jj Kk Ll Mn Nn
Oo Pp Qq Rr Ss Tt **Uu** Vv Ww Xx Yy Zz

We use *capital letters*....
with towns and cities	London; **B**eijing; **T**okyo; **K**uala **L**umpur
with countries	**S**audi **A**rabia; **S**outh **K**orea; **Y**emen;
with nationalities	**L**ibyan; **D**jiboutian; **M**ongolian

Write the *preposition*:
at	+ school; university
	Ahmed is studying **at** A Language School.
from	China
	She's **from** China
	+ city/country
	London
in	London is **in** England.
on	They're **on** holiday.

Write the correct *preposition* in the space.

1. I'll have lunch _____ work.

2. Where's Tokyo. It's _____ Japan,.

3. I don't live _____ a flat. I live _____ a house..

4. I go to work _____ my bicycle.

5. I got a letter _____ my mum.

Re - write the sentences with capital letters.
1. thiery henri is a french footballer. _____

_____

2. beijing is the capital city of china. _____

_____

3. where is virginia from? I think she's spanish. _____

_____

4. seoul is a big city in south korea. _____

_____

5. i'm 22 and I'm turkish _____

_____

Complete the sentences with *PREPOSITIONS* that describe the pictures.
Write each *preposition* – once. (using the *capital letter*)
A bear is _____ Aishah's legs. (and others)

A- next to; B-in; C-in front of; D-on; E-above/below; F-between

Prepositions

1. My best friend lives _____ Malaysia.
   a. on
   b. in
   c. at

2. Since he met his new friend, he doesn't seem to be _____ home
   a. at
   b. with
   c. on

3. I'll be ready to leave _____ a few minutes.
   a. on
   b. in
   c. since

4. The child responded to her mother's demands, _____ a tantrum.
   a. on
   b. about
   c. with

5. I think she spends all her time _____ the phone.
   a. on
   b. in
   c. at

5. I will wait _____ 9.30, but then I'm going home.
   a. in
   b. until
   c. at

6. The constable caught the thief _____ the corner of the post office.
   a. about
   b. in
   c. at

Instructions:- For each question, choose the best single answer.

8. I couldn't come so my dad wrote a note _____ me.
   a. by
   b. for
   c. at

9. I'm not interested _____ buying a new car now.
   a. in
   b. for
   c. on

10. What are the ingredients _____ this cake?
    a. about
    b. to
    c. in

11. My daughter is named _____ one the Prophet's wives.
    a. with
    b. for
    c. after

12. I stayed up to watch TV _____ two in the morning.
    a. in
    b. for
    c. until

13. Students learn English _____ enroll into a university.
    a. to
    b. in
    c. by

14. You can buy things _____ a credit card.
    a. on
    b. at
    c. with

A, An, The

_____   _____   _____   _____

Write the following names under the above pictures:-
1. the exercise bike   2.a chair   3.a rabbit   4.an elephant

An – is used as a pre-fix before nouns that begin with **a, e, i, o, u**
These are called VOWELS
We use it for singular or countable nouns that begin with the above letters.
They are also used because of the way they sound.
A – is used as a pre-fix before nouns that begin with all the other letters.
These are called CONSONANTS
We use it for singular or countable nouns that don't begin with the above letters.
They are also used because of the way they sound.
However, there are some words that don't sound like they should.
They look like something and sound different.

hour

honour } both have their first letter sounding like a vowel **NOT** a *consonant.*

universe

unity } both have their first letter sounding like a *consonant* **NOT** a *vowel*
                    U sounds like **you**

Therefore, when speaking   –   " It' an honor to meet you."
                                                      "See you in an hour."
                                                      "We are studying in a university."

These are called *indefinite articles*
If we speak about all *nouns, vowels and consonants,* for a second time, we promote them
To **THE**
The man.   *The* woman.   *The* orange.   *The* anniversary
Or, if there is only one of a kind, of anything.
The Pacific Ocean   The sky   The moon   The earth
These are called *definite articles*

CAPITAL *LETTERS* / *Articles*

Aa Bb Cc Dd **Ee** Ff Gg Hh **Ii** Jj Kk Ll Mn Nn
Oo Pp Qq Rr Ss Tt **Uu** Vv Ww Xx Yy Zz

The above large letters are called capital letters, upper-case. The smaller letters are called lower-case. The letters in **bold** are called *vowels*. The rest are called *consonants*.

We use *capital letters*….
with names   Jackie Chan;   Michael Jackson

at the beginning of a sentence   Hello. **My** name's **Paul**. What's your name?

with I   **I'm** James.

Write *a / an / the* in the correct place.

1. Could I have _____ drink of water please?

2. I'm staying in _____ small hotel. _____ one over there.

3. _____ hotel around the corner, doesn't, have _____ en-suite I need.

4. It's raining. I must take _____ umbrella. When I walk back to _____ car.

5. They say _____ apple _____ day, will keep _____ doctor away.

Re - write the sentences with *capital letters*.

a. his name's tony. he's an actor. _____

b. my name's phil. i'm a teacher. _____

c. they're famous. they're from italy. _____

d. hello mohammed, how are you? _____

e. her name's wendy. she's a dancer. _____

I Want to Be a Good Student

Change small letters to capital letters and punctuate wherever necessary in the following essay.

Make **class,** **mustn't**
~~make~~ make sure you pay attention in ~~class~~ class you mustn't start talking on your
mobile,
friends or be on your ~~mobile~~ mobile especially when your teachers turn their backs to
you.
~~you~~

you also must not be involved with distracting people you should understand that the people in your class play an important role in how you and everybody else progresses however, if you are a good student you can do better and achieve your goals your friends will be much more appreciative of you, if you show a good example at home, study and do your homework in a place that doesn't make you sleep stay away from the tv / radio/and stereos however some students find soothing music a benefit it is also advisable to have a study table or desk in a room designated for studying this would be a very good idea because it will help you concentrate on your studies

if you feel distracted, take a short break of 15 minutes or less maybe try to read an unrelated story book. but don't get hooked to the book if the time limit is over book mark the page and then you can read it later on you should also have a daily routine/timetable to guide you, but you must follow it through

dont cheat by copying from your colleagues....always remember cheating will make you lose....your friends answer may not always be the right answer, it could be wrong. its best therefore to go with your first instinctive idea you will probably find that if you have faith in your own abilities…it will usually be the correct answer dont cheat be honest if you dont know the answer leave it dont dwell on a question; move on if you are not sure make sure you try to answer all the questions in an exam exams are set up for students to also test their time management as well as their knowledge return to questions you are unsure, when you have initially finished an exam remember, study well now and you can have fun after you achieve your goal – guaranteed good luck

Chapter Two

Titles
and
Topics

Titles & Topics

A *title* can be :-

i)   the name of a book: ***How to Play the Saxophone***

2)   the name of a film   ***Wuthering Heights***

3)   a piece of music: ***Swan Lake***

4)   a word in front of   ***Sir*** *Nick Faldo*
        someone's name:

The *title* however, need not be directly associated with *topic*, but must have some kind of connection. For example:-

i)   ***My Family***
        Topic 1)   ***My Parents***
        Topic 2)   ***My Siblings***
ii)   ***Cats***
        Topic 1)   ***Wild Cats***
        Topic 2)   ***Domesticated Cats***

Put the *titles* and *topics* in their respective places.

1.   ***Food; Vegetables; Fruit.***
        (carrots; cauliflower; onions; apple; pear; banana; strawberries; cherries; orange)

        _____

        Topic 1)   _____

        Topic 2)   _____
                            (see page 13)

2.   ***Things with many parts; Rooms in a House; Bicycle Parts:***
        (kitchen; handlebars; bedroom; saddle; bathroom;
        wheel; lounge; brakes)

        _____

        Topic 1)   _____

        Topic 2)   _____
                            (see page 14)

Understanding *Topics*

Topics That Are Names of Groups

What is a *topic*? A *topic* tells what something is about the title. It helps readers remember the title they have chosen. There are two kinds of *topics*. One kind is **the name of a group of things**

...........**FOOD** (1. page 12)

the other kind is **the name of a thing with many parts.**

...........**ROOMS in a HOUSE and BICYCLE PARTS** (2. page 12)

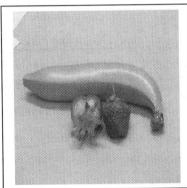

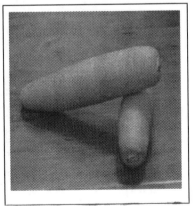

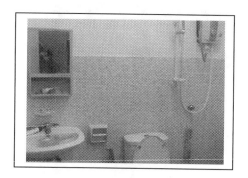

Finding Group *Topics*

Find the *topic* title for each group of words. Write it on the line above.
Then think of another associated word. Write in it the space alongside.

1.   *Topic:-* **The House Garden** _____   **flowers**

     trees   bushes   fountain   grass   birds

2.   *Topic:-* _____   _____

     nose   ears   forehead   chin   cheek

3.   *Topic:-* _____   _____

     meat   cheese   bread   vegetables   fruit

4.   *Topic:-* _____   _____

     soda   tea   coffee   water   sugar

5.   *Topic:-* _____   _____

     car   bus   train   bicycle   plane

6.   *Topic:-* _____   _____

     grand-father niece   uncle   brother   nephew

7.   *Topic:-* _____   _____

     morning   evening   midnight   night   dawn

8.   *Topic:-* _____   _____

     book   magazine   comic   poem   newspaper

9.   *Topic:-* _____   _____

     thirty-nine three   twenty-one   fifteen   six

10. *Topic:-* _____   _____

     feet   arms   shoulders   chest   hands

Being Organised When Writing

Having a good organisation sense about wring is the key to having your work understood. Many languages divide up their ideas differently and that is why it's important to arrange paragraphs, so that they flow, in an orderly fashion. We can start by organizing places into groups.

Look at the list of places around the world in the list below. How are we going to put them in a logical order? First let's see if any of them are similar in any way.

Divide them into three groups.

Mexico

Portugal

Paris

Wellington

South America

Europe

London

Malaysia

Asia

A	B	C
Europe_____	Malaysia_____	Paris_____
_____	_____	_____
_____	_____	_____

1. What do all the places in group **A** have in common?

   _____

2. What do all the places in group **B** have in common?

   _____

3. What do all the places in group **C** have in common?

   _____

Organising Lists

Organise each of the following lists by dividing them into three groups.
Give each group a name

1. Tuesday   December
    Autumn   June
    September   Saturday
    Summer   Spring
    Friday   Spring

    A   B   C

    Name_____   Name_____   Name_____

    _____   _____   _____

    _____   _____   _____

    _____   _____   _____

2. jet   truck
    bus   helicopter
    boat   sub-marine
    car   ship
    aeroplane

    A   B   C

    Name_____   Name_____   Name_____

    _____   _____   _____

    _____   _____   _____

    _____   _____   _____

Organising Lists

Organise each list item into groups of two and then sub groups of four. They will then

3. champagne   broccoli   chicken
    beef   whiskey   lemon tea
    carrots   lamb   beer
    lemonade   potatoes   milk

Add extra items to the final lists.

A

Name_____

_____

_____

_____

_____

_____

_____

B

Name_____

_____

_____

_____

_____

_____

_____

A

Name_____

_____

_____

_____

_____

B

Name _____

_____

_____

_____

_____

C

Name_____

_____

_____

_____

_____

D

Name_____

_____

_____

_____

_____

Chapter Three

Introductory Paragraphs

The Introductory Paragraph

The first paragraph in an essay is very important. It is composed of sentences that will lead the reader into what the rest of the essay is about. A good introduction will entice the reader to read on, a window that will open the mind further. Therefore the introduction has a double purpose, to introduce the essay topic to the readers and to get their attention.

The paragraph has to be very general. Not to be specific and to this end, use words and phrases that are non-specific. That means not using *pronouns* such as my; our; their; your; his and her. Other *determiners* are used such as many; some; quite a few and not many. These are general and non-specific and will not give a direct viewpoint to any chosen topic.

Question words are very helpful in deciding the usage of *determiners* in an *introductory paragraph*. They can also be used to construct sentences in all *paragraphs*.

Question - words	Usage	Example	Responses
1. *Where* (area)	Asks about the place of an event or action.	i. *Where* do you come from? ii. *Where* is my pen?	-I come from England. -I think it's here.
2. *Who* (person/s)	Asks about people.	i. *Who* is that boy? ii. *Who* does he work for?	-He's my son. -He works for a big firm.
3. *Which* (sort)	Asks about people and things.	i. *Which* one is his? ii. *Which* of these are hers?	-The blue one, I think. -The one with the redtop.
4. *Why* (reason)	Asks about the views and opinions.	i. *Why* are we here? ii. *Why* did you leave it at home.?	-We have to register. -I didn't need it.
5. *When* (time)	Asks about the time of the event.	i. *When* is it? ii. *When* are the exams?	-I think it's today. -They're on Monday
6. *How* (method)	Asks about the manner in which an action is performed.	i. *How* are you ? ii. *How* are we getting home?	-Much better, thanks. -We are going by train then a taxi.
7. *What* (subject)	Asks about people animals and things	i. *What* is his pet? ii. *What* are your skills?	-It's a tortoise. -I can cook and play the guitar.

Exercises

Circle the best answer.

1. _____ is the book?
   - a. When
   - b. Where
   - c. Why
   - d. How

2. _____ is your father's occupation?
   - a. When
   - b. What
   - c. Why
   - d. Who

3. _____ is the toy? It is in the living room
   - a. When
   - b. Where
   - c. Why
   - d. How

4. _____ is your mother?
   - a. When
   - b. What
   - c. Why
   - d. How

5. _____ did you get here?
   - a. Who
   - b. Where
   - c. What
   - d. How

6. _____ are you studying? The English language.
   - a. When
   - b. What
   - c. Why
   - d. How

7. _____ will you come home? Today, I think.
   - a. When
   - b. Where
   - c. Why
   - d. What

8. _____ are you feeling?
   - a. When
   - b. Where
   - c. Why
   - d. How

9. _____ are you phoning? My dad.
   - a. Who
   - b. Where
   - c. Why
   - d. How

10. _____ is the bank?
    - a. When
    - b. Where
    - c. Why
    - d. How

11. _____ are you doing?
    - a. When
    - b. Where
    - c. Why
    - d. What

12. _____ is it closing? At 3.00 pm.
    - a. When
    - b. Why
    - c. Where
    - d. How

13. _____ are you coming?
    - a. When
    - b. Why
    - c. Where
    - d. How

14. _____ is that man? That's my brother
    - a. When
    - b. Why
    - c. Who
    - d. How

15. _____ is the exam room?
    - a. When
    - b. Why
    - c. Where
    - d. How

16. _____ is the time please?
    - a. When
    - b. What
    - c. Who
    - d. How

17. _____ are you coming? Because I have to go shopping.
    - a. When
    - b. Why
    - c. Who
    - d. How

18. _____ are you feeling? Very well, thank you.
    - a. When
    - b. Where
    - c. Why
    - d. How

Quantifiers: *a few - many*   *a little - much*

Countable	**Uncountable**
Many glasses	*Much* money
A *few* cookies	A *little* amount of honey
Many containers	Not *much* milk
A *few* mugs	Just a *little* amount of salt

Complete the sentences with *a few/ many* or *a little / much*

1. My grandmother has made so _____ jars of jam for all of us..

2. There is _____ milk in the fridge.

3. They only drank _____ cans on holiday.

4. There aren't _____ bears left now.

5. I haven't got_____ money left now.

6. Are there _____ balloons to be blown up?

7. Please buy _____ to put on the toast.

8. We only ate _____ cookies before tea.

9. All you need is_____ to add to the soup.

10. _____ of us are going to go out tonight.

Introduction Paragraph Construction
Title

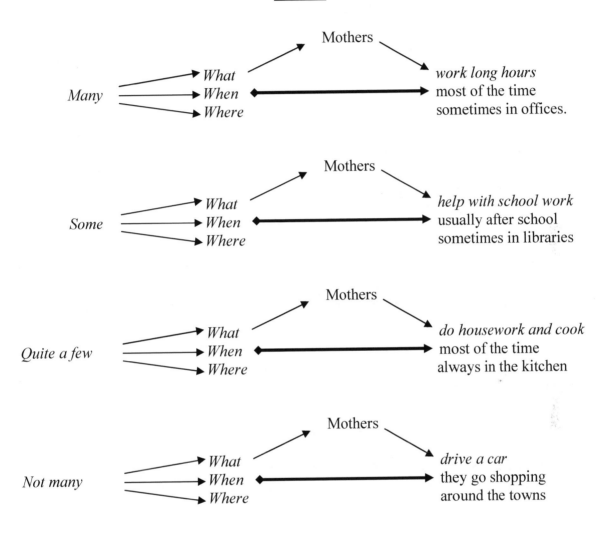

Many → What → Mothers → work long hours
When ➤ most of the time
Where → sometimes in offices.

Some → What → Mothers → help with school work
When ➤ usually after school
Where → sometimes in libraries

Quite a few → What → Mothers → do housework and cook
When ➤ most of the time
Where → always in the kitchen

Not many → What → Mothers → drive a car
When ➤ they go shopping
Where → around the towns

Introduction Paragraph Construction

Write the *titles* that you choose and construct the *Introduction Paragraphs.*
Refer to the sample on **page 23.**

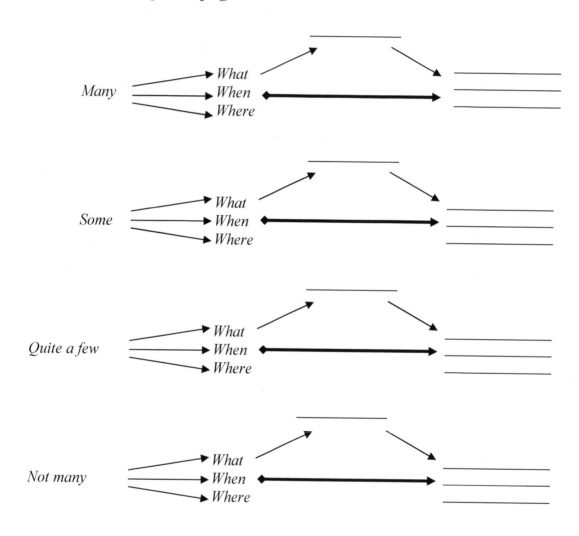

Titles and Introductions

Parents

My Family

Siblings

The *fathers* and *mothers* are the backbone to any family. *The siblings,* if any, also help to bond the family unit together. The *father usually* makes the decisions. *Mothers* will *always* maintain an orderly house. The *father rarely* cleans the house but *sometimes* might cook. The *siblings,* when able will also help share in house duties.

London

My City and Kuala Lumpur

Beijing

Many cities have similar buildings. *Some* people of similar cities speak the same language. *A lot of* cities have rivers flowing through them. *Quite a few* cities have famous statues and buildings in them.

Good Holiday

My Holiday

Bad Holiday

Many people go, or would like to go on a holiday. There are *many* reasons for doing so. They may be personal or just for the experience. When they return, *most* people will have unforgettable experiences. *Some* people will have good times to remember. However, others will not be so fortunate.

Singers

A Chosen Celebrity

Actors / Actresses

Celebrities are such because they are famous. *Many* would not be called such if a few people knew them. *However* even though they could be world-known, they might non-entities to *some* people. They are *usually* recognized when they come on TV. This is because of the exposure they will receive. Actors, actresses and sportsmen will *always* be recognized as well as singers and pop-stars.

Titles and *Introductions*

My Parents

_____

_____

_____

_____

My City and London

_____

_____

_____

_____

How to Drive Your Parents Crazy

_____

_____

_____

_____

Chosen Actor/Actress

_____

_____

_____

_____

Chapter Four

The

Thesis

Statements

Rules for *Thesis Statements* (propositions or dissertations)

1. A *thesis statement* must be a statement, **NOT a question.**

2. A *thesis statement* must be a complete sentence. This means that it must have a **subject and a verb.**

3. A *thesis statement* **cannot be a simple statement of *fact.*** A *fact* doesn't need any support, therefore you cannot write an essay about it.

4. A *thesis statement* must **state the controlling idea,** not just wonder whether or not if something is true. This means that you must state your position on the *topic*; you simply cannot make an announcement of what you are going to write in the essay.

5. A *thesis statement* should have **one controlling idea;** not several different ones.

- Which of the sentences below are *thesis statements?*
- Put a check mark (✓) next to those you think are *thesis statements.*
- If you think the sentence is not a *thesis sentence*, write the number of the rule it violates, in the box, next to it.

A	Japanese cars are better than American cars.	
B	A Proton is a Malaysian car.	
C	I am going to show you that seat belts are necessary.	
D	Are seat belts necessary?	
E	Seat belts save lives and money	

28

Thesis Statement Construction

Sometimes, a subject has to go through several stages of limiting, before it is narrow enough to write. Below are four lists that writers went through before narrowing them down to a *thesis statement*. Put each list in order of rank. This is to help identify the priority in writing the subjects of the main point, that culminates into the broader points of the *title*.

List One   **List Two**

_____Teachers   _____Bicycles

1
_____Education   _____Dangers of
                                                                                                            bike riding

_____Professors   _____Recreation

                                                                                        2
_____Good and bad   _____Recreational
             mathematics teachers   vehicles

_____High School   _____Advantages and
             Mathematics teachers   disadvantages
                                                                                                            of bike riding

List Three   **List Four**

_____Advantages and   _____Camping
             disadvantages of
             working in a bank.   **4**

_____Bank   _____First camping trip

_____Dealing with customers   _____Summer vacation

3
_____Working in a bank.   _____Vacations

_____Financial Institutions   _____Advantages and
                                                                                                            disadvantages
                                                                                                            of camping

29

The *Thesis Statement*

There are many ideas on how a good *thesis statement* should be composed. The writer should decide on whether they want to construct a weak or strong one. For the benefit of new students, I am only going to concentrate *on thesis statements* that you not only understand but are able to construct easily yourselves. When you get to the higher levels you may want to elaborate further.

The important thing to remember is that your *thesis* needs to show conclusions about a subject. The composition, like the paragraph, is controlled by one central idea. *It* is a one-sentence summary of the whole composition.

Here are some examples of *thesis statements*:-

1. This essay will discuss the *advantages and disadvantages* of having parents and siblings

2. In this essay I will discuss the *advantages and disadvantages* of having lived in two countries.

3. There are both *advantages and disadvantages* of living away from home.

4. There are advantages and disadvantages to owning your own car

5. In this essay I will discuss the *advantages and disadvantages* of being married.

Thesis statements can also allow the writer to write two sub-*topic sentences* that can have paragraphs relating to the main *topic*.

For example:-

1. My **parents** are always supportive in what I do.

   My **father** is a hardworking man.

   My **mother** is a very good cook.

2. My **siblings** are very good sports people.

   My **brothers** play football.

   My **sisters** are in the volleyball and netball teams.

The Difference Between a *Thesis Statement* and a *Topic Sentence.*

The **thesis statement** (*sentence)* governs the whole content of the whole composition, whereas the **topic sentence** governs the development of *one paragraph.*
It also points to a landmark or landmarks along the way.

Thesis statements, point to the ultimate destination, of an essay.

Example 1 :-*SUBJECT*	*VERB*	*TOPIC*
This essay	will discuss	the *advantages and disadvantages of owning a car.*

Example 2 :-*SUBJECT*	*VERB*	*TOPIC*
In this essay I	will discuss	the *advantages and disadvantages* of being married.

Example 3 :-*SUBJECT*	*VERB*	*TOPIC*
There	are	*advantages and disadvantages* of living away from home.

Topic sentences, should introduce the main idea of the paragraph.

	SUBJECT	*VERB*	*OPINION*	*TOPIC*
Body	i) There	are	many *advantages*	of owning a car.
Paragraph 1	ii) Owning a car	has	several	*advantages.*
	iii) There	are	many positive aspects to owning a car.	

Look, forward, to pages **47-49,** to see how *transition signals* can be used to emphasize the differences between **the** *topics*.

Body Paragraph 2	i)	However, owning a car	has	also many	*disadvantages*
	ii)	However, there	are	also many negative aspects	to owning a car.
	iii)	There	are	also several *disadvantages*	to owning a car

More Examples 0f Differences Between
Thesis Statements and *Topic Sentences.*

Write *your own* **topic** examples in the spaces provided:-

Example :-	*SUBJECT*	*VERB*	*TOPIC*
	This essay	will discuss	the **advantages** *and* **disadvantages** of owning a car

	:-	*SUBJECT*	*VERB*	*TOPIC*

a) _____

b) _____

c) _____

Topic sentences:- should introduce the main ideas of the paragraph.

SUBJECT:-   is what we should talk about

TOPIC:-   are the main points of the SUBJECT

		SUBJECT	*VERB*	*OPINION*	*TOPIC*
Body Paragraph 1	i)	Owning a car	has	many	**advantages**

d) _____

e) _____

f) _____

		SUBJECT	*VERB*	*OPINION*	*TOPIC*
Body Paragraph 2	ii)	However, owning a car.	has	also many	**disadvantages**

g) _____

h) _____

i) _____

Chapter Five

Topic Sentences

Topic Sentences

A paragraph is a group of sentences about the same *topic*. The main idea about the paragraph should be given in the first sentence. This sentence is called the *topic sentence*. It introduces the *subject* matter, to be discussed and the information to be given to the other sentences.

Constructing *Topic Sentences*

Topic sentences are constructed directly from the title. They are related to the *title* but may not necessarily be constructed using the same vocabulary. There are two ways of constructing *topic sentences*. Using the *title* or from *supporting sentences*. In an exam the former is sometimes the best method, but if you have time, the main crux of a story can be used.

We use the *Wh-* words in order to give us some idea for the *topic sentence*.

Add another question of your own, to the following.

	Title	My Father

Ex 1   Wh –**at**
(subject)

What job does he do? **What** time does he go to work?
What time does he come home?

*What*_____

Wh-**y**
(reason)

Why does he leave at a particular time? **Why** does he work at a particular place?

*Why*_____

Wh-**en**
(time)

When did he start working there? **When** does he have time to relax?
When does he find time to be with his family?

*When*_____

Wh-**ere**
(place)

Where does he work? **Where** does he go to relax?

*Where*_____

Wh-**o**
(person/s)

Who does he work with? **Who** does he relax with?

*Who*_____

How
(method)

How does he get there and home? **How** does he relax?

*How*_____

Ex 2. There are twelve supporting ideas for the *topic sentence*. Now we will use the answers to construct a *topic sentence*.

Use one or two word answers.

What job does he do?

Doctor_____   _____

Why does he leave at a particular

time?

Early practice_____   _____

When did he start working there?

Ten years ago_____   _____

Where does he work?

In town_____   _____

Who does he work with?

Two doctors _____   _____

How does he get to work ?

By bus_____   _____

My father is a hardworking doctor.

My father	is	hardworking	doctor
SUBJECT	*VERB*	*OPINION*	*TOPIC*

Notice how the *topic sentence* is formed.

Write a sentence using your own answers.

_____

The latter, *supporting sentences*, are formed from the above as well.

1.   He leaves work very early.

2.   He started working there ten years ago.

3.   He works in town with two other doctors.

4.   He travels every day by bus.

Creating *Topic* Sentences **ONE Paragraph**

Title	Subject	Verb	Opinion	Topic
My Family	My family	Is		
My Parents	My Parents			
My Father	My father	Is		
My Mother	My mother	Is		
My Siblings	My siblings	are		
My Brother	My brother (s)			
My Sister	My sister	Is/are		

TWO Paragraphs

Title	Subject	Verb	Opinion	Topic
My Family	My parents My siblings	are		
My Parents	My father My mother	is		
My Siblings	My brother (s) My sister (s)	Is/are		
My Brother	My elder brothers My younger brothers	are		
My Sister	My elder sisters My younger sisters	are		
My Grandparents My Uncle/Aunts	My grandparents My uncle/aunt(s)	are		

Topic Sentence Construction

From the following two paragraphs, construct the *Topic Sentence*. Read the paragraph carefully and answer the three Wh-questions. Remember how the *Topic Sentence* is formed, (use one or two words for your answers).

One of the penguins was ready to play. He waddled up the icy hill as fast as he could. Then he flopped onto his stomach and slid. Some of the penguins were eating lunch. They swallowed the fish as quickly as the zookeeper could empty the buckets of food. A few of the penguins were sleeping quietly. The children watch the penguins for a long time. When it was time to go, the children were sad. Many of the children liked the penguin exhibit the best.

1.   *What* _____?
2.   *Where* _____?
3.   *Who* _____?

a.   Write a *topic sentence*, using your answers

SUBJECT   ***VERB***   ***OPINION***   ***TOPIC***

_____

The students of Mrs. Jones's class were having a great time at the Zoo. Mrs. Jones suddenly remembered as they passed a restaurant sign, it was getting late and the children hadn't eaten. "Has anyone got the time"? She asked. Jimmy looked at his watch. "It's 1.50", he said. "Oh no! We're supposed to meet Mr. Smith's class at 1.30. We're late!" They all started running towards the entrance.

1.   *What* _____?
2.   *When* _____?
3.   *Who* _____?

a.   Write a *topic sentence,* using your answers

SUBJECT   ***VERB***   ***OPINION***   ***TOPIC***

_____

Choosing Topic Sentences

Notice that ALL the support sentences relate to the *topic sentence*. Read the paragraphs and then answer the questions that follow.

1. There are many reasons why many of people move from their countries every year. Some move to find better jobs to advance their careers. Others are attracted to countries or places with better climates. Others may move because of an increasing level of violence. The reduced cost of living could also be a factor.

   What is the topic sentence? _____

   _____

   Do all the *supporting sentences* relate to the *topic sentence*? YES / NO _____

2. Many men are now employed in what were traditionally, the jobs of women. For example, there are now twice as many male nurses as there were in 1990. Since 1992, the number of male telephone operators has almost trebled. Also, the number of male secretaries has increased by twenty-four percent.

   What is the topic sentence? _____

   _____

   Do all the *supporting sentences* relate to the *topic sentence*? YES / NO _____

3. Garlic has had its uses throughout history. The Romans gave it to their slaves. Witches were kept away by its use, in the Middle ages. In the 18th century, it was used to cure diseases. Some people still think that by eating it will prevent colds.

   What is the topic sentence? _____

   _____

   Do all the *supporting sentences* relate to the *topic sentence*? YES / NO _____

4. Video games have become popular in some college campuses. Most colleges have at least one video game. These games can make a lot of money a term for colleges. The colleges use the money to improve the college facilities.

   What is the topic sentence? _____

   _____

   Do all the *supporting sentences* relate to the *topic sentence*? YES / NO _____

Choosing a *Topic Sentence*

*Choose the best **topic sentences** for each of the following paragraphs and write them on the lines provided.*

1).   a.   Rates and taxes should be enlarged
      b.   The council needs money to repair the coaches.
      c.   The government has lots of cash.

Many of the coaches need repair work. Councillors tell everyone that there is not enough money to repair them. The council will have to get money from the government

_____

2).   a.   Shopping is difficult.
      b.   The supermarkets are very busy on particular days.
      c.   It is wise to do special day shopping earlier.

It will be difficult if you wait just before special days. Many supermarkets run out of the most popular items, so it will be harder to find what you want. The supermarkets will also be crowded and waiting lines are much longer.

_____

3).   a.   Skiing is expensive.
      b.   Skiing is loved by a lot of people.
      c.   There are many problems to skiing.

Many people enjoy skiing, even though it's expensive and dangerous. A lot of people attend week-end skiing every winter. Many families go on skiing holidays. Neither the high cost of skiing or equipment deters skiers away from the slopes.

_____

4).   a.   Travelling in the air has altered our lives.
      b.   Advances in technology have made the world seem reduced in size.
      c.   An important invention was the mobile phone.

A person can have a breakfast in Sydney, board a plane and have dinner in Singapore. A businessman in Kuala Lumpur can instantly place an order in Taiwan by picking up a telephone. A schoolboy in China can watch his favorite soccer team playing in London, on television.

_____

Title and Topic Sentences

Write a *title* for each story and change the *topic sentence (in* italics) to one of your own.
(see pages 34 and 35)

1).

_____

_____

_____

Jane is driving her new car, it will make her life more comfortable. She has soft leather seats and a back- rest. There is a wide view mirror, so that she can see all around her, although she hasn't got automatic gears. The interior is quite spacious and all her family can go with her. She won't have to wait for the bus anymore so that Jane won't have to carry her shopping long distances.

2).

_____

_____

_____

The family has a new bathroom and everyone is pleased. Dad has a new shaving mirror, that comes out from the wall and mum has got her hairdryer fixed. Susan has her own cabinet and although the boys have not got a jacuzzi, they have a new shower.

3).

_____

_____

_____

There is a new playground in the park There is a roundabout and three swings. There is also a slide for big children and a small one for the toddlers. A see-saw has a double-seat at each end and although there is no monkey-tree, the children can climb in and out of some apparatus.

Chapter Six

Irrelevant

Sentences

SUPPORTING SENTENCES Recognising Irrelevant *Sentences*

Many students, when writing essays, waste a lot of time writing sentences that are totally un-related to the *topic* of the sentence. They are totally irrelevant. You must be focused upon the *topic* otherwise you get sidetracked away from your purpose. Write the *topic* on the line; cross out the irrelevant one and write a suitable one on the line above.

1.   *Topic* __**Drinks**__   __**coffee**__

           orange juice   tea   hot chocolate   ~~sugar~~ lemonade

It does not belong, because **sugar is not a drink.**

2.   *Topic* _____   _____

       rabbit   budgerigar   tiger   goldfish   hamster

It does not belong, because_____

3.   *Topic* _____   _____

       study   kitchen   sitting room   garden   hall

It does not belong, because_____

4.   *Topic* _____   _____

       Tokyo   England   Somalia   Sudan   Libya

It does not belong, because_____

5.   *Topic* _____   _____

       fifteen   thirty-five   twenty-seven   sixty   fourty-five

It does not belong, because_____

SUPPORTING SENTENCES *Recognising Irrelevant Sentences*

The following paragraphs contain one sentence that is **irrelevant**. Cross out the ***irrelevant*** one and explain why it should not be there.

1.   Cats make wonderful pets. They are loving and friendly. They are also clean. They don't eat much so they are inexpensive. ***Some have short tails.*** They look beautiful. However some people are allergic to their hair.

It ***does not belong*** because ***having short tails isn't a reason why they should make good pets.***

2.   Learning the English language has many *advantages*. Most people in many countries speak it. Therefore it's a good communication tool. It's widely used on the internet. My grandmother now speaks it. Many textbooks are written in English.

It *does not* belong, because_____

_____

3.   Exercising has many positive effects on the body. First, it increases the efficiency of many body organs. Many people prefer to diet. Next, it will improve the physical endurance capabilities. Finally, this will increase the chances of wearing nice clothes.

It *does not* belong, because_____

_____

4.   The Korean automobile industry uses robots in many phases of its industry. In fact, one large Korean auto factory is now using robots in all of its production. Some Japanese universities are developing medical robots to detect certain kinds of cancer. Some Japanese factories are using robots to paint their cars. Others are using them to test-drive.

It *does not* belong, because_____

_____

5.   There are a lot of reasons why women are waiting until they are thirty-plus to have their first baby. Some have good jobs and want to continue their careers. Others don't want the responsibility. Many couples already have children. A few have seen how it ruined marriages.

It *does not* belong, because_____

Features of an *Irrelevant Topic Sentence* (exercises)

Exercise 1._____(refer to page 28)
Read the following sentences and decide if they are *facts* or *opinions*.

~~Cross out the~~ wrong one.

1,	An apartment is a set of rooms that are usually on the same level.	Fact / Opinion.
2.	It's better to live on the highest floor.	Fact / Opinion.
3.	A detached house is not one that is joined to another house.	Fact / Opinion.
4.	Our apartment overlooked a small courtyard.	Fact / Opinion.
5.	The neighbor's house had a rather nice bay window.	Fact / Opinion.
6.	I don't think there was anyone living in the basement.	Fact / Opinion.
7.	The housing estate is an area where there are a lot of houses.	Fact / Opinion.
8.	The landlord is someone that you rent the house or flat from.	Fact / Opinion.
9.	My landlord is a very fair person.	Fact / Opinion.
10.	Our apartment is on the third floor.	Fact / Opinion.

Exercise 2
Read each *topic sentence* and put a ✓ next to the ideas that are suitable
and a ✗ next to the ideas that are not.

1. My mother is always a hardworking woman.

_____	cleans the house every day.	_____	likes baking cakes
_____	goes shopping at week-ends.	_____	sleeps very late.
_____	helps us with our homework.	_____	cooks all the meals

2. The library is a good place to read books.

_____	it helps gain knowledge.	_____	must have good eyesight
_____	saves money by renting	_____	improves vocabulary
_____	can read, anytime, anyplace	_____	can be hard or soft back

3. In the home useful animals are usually dogs.

_____	guard the house	_____	smell out drugs
_____	eat what they are given	_____	track missing people
_____	can do tricks	_____	loyal to their masters

Chapter Seven

Supporting

Sentences

Identifying Topic and Supporting Sentences

Supporting sentences are what the name implies. They not only support the *topic sentences* but also the *concluding sentences*. Therefore they must be seen to be *linking* the two together.

Supporting sentences must have a direct correlation with the *topic*. They must not deviate away from its essence otherwise the true meaning of the *paragraph* will not only be lost, but will also be ambiguous.

There are two ways that this can be avoided. First, *signal* words can be used in order to direct the reader from start to finish. They will not only help the writer but also the reader to understand what is going on. This method is used when writing about a *topic* with similar intentions and results.

Page forty-eight illustrates this very well. When writing about something you have done or are about to do, it's very helpful to picture the events as you write. Having been to or done something yourself, will *always* be helpful when writing.

After writing a title (remember to *capitalize* the words correctly, pages three and four), number the pictures, you think should be in order Then complete the *linking sentences* and write a *paragraph.*

Signal words may be adopted, but breaking up the first two *supporting sentences* further is more effective. This method also ensures that the writer has a better flow of information and direction. There is little danger of the reader being pulled away by *irrelevant sentences* (discussed in the previous chapter) Use the *Wh- words*, (discussed in chapter three) when mind-mapping, to formulate the *supporting sentences*. When you pre-plan an essay this way, every *title/topic* will become as familiar as getting dressed.

Words that Signal a Text's Organisational Structure.

Students sometimes struggle to organize their notes to answer research questions. It might help them if they can understand certain words.

- **In the case of a research question**, students should begin on deciding on what type of question they need to answer.
- **In the case of a reading assignment**, the passage should be determined, early, on how it is to be organised.
- **In both cases**, students can look for some of the original *signal words* listed below, in helping them make up their minds.

Here is a list of *Signal Words*:-

Chronological Sequence
after first afterward initially
next following immediately
finally until as soon as before
then now when meanwhile
not long after third on
preceding

Generalisation / Principle
additionally most convincing how
to moreover conclusively is
caused by typically in order to
for this reason
effects of if...then steps
involved not only but also
furthermore

Process / Cause and Effect
accordingly as a result of always first clearly
conclusively furthermore generally however
if...then in fact truly never
it could be argued that typically most
convincing third second
not only but...also typically

Comparison / Contrast
but as well as opposed to yet
on although compared still
on the other hand in common
different from however
similar to even though

Description
above along across
back / front of appears to be as in behind
below to the right/left over into under
between near down beside on top of outside

47

Linking Sentences

The flow of a story can always be helped by the aid of *conjunction* words. Choose the correct *linking* word and write another sentence using the same word.
Then finish off the sentences from F – M.

A) We will visit England. .... Scotland next year.
    i) and   ii) but   iii) therefore

_____ ...._____

B) My back was aching. ....I went to see my doctor.
    i) and   ii) but   iii) so

_____ ...._____

C) I wanted to go skiing. ....I couldn't get a flight in time.
    i) but   ii) so   iii) therefore

_____ ...._____

D) My brother wanted something to eat. ....he went and bought a sandwich.
    i) therefore   i) and   iii) so

_____ ...._____

E) I want to pass my exams. ....I am always going to do my homework.
    i) and   ii) but   iii) so

_____ ...._____

F) It was very expensive, but_____

G) They never come on time, so_____

H) It's a very expensive restaurant and_____

I) It didn't look good, so_____

J) It's snowing, but_____

K) It's open late. so_____

L) I'd love to help and_____

M) There's a train strike but_____

Using Linking and Signal Words

You often, find it difficult to keep your thoughts in order. Initially when writing paragraphs, it is sometimes best to use words that help you write, in a sequential manner. Write a *title,* put the numbers sequentially against the appropriate pictures. Then write your own sentences in the correct sequence. Use the *linking* words, on page 48, to construct a paragraph. Use the un-numbered pictures for additional ideas. For example, give a reason why she is running late for her bus.

Identifying Topic and Supporting Sentences

A *Read the following sentences about Springfield Academy, a boarding school for high-school students. There is too much information for one paragraph. Some of the sentences are about the **q**uality of the education and some are about the **r**ules of the school. Label the former **Q** and the latter **R**.*

1. _____ The laboratories have the latest equipment.

2. _____ Students are not allowed to leave without permission.

3. _____ Students are required to wear uniforms.

4. _____ Therefore, having the best equipment ensures best results.

5. _____ The Academy is famous for its quality education.

6. _____ Most of its graduates attend very good universities.

7. _____ many of the students of The Academy feel that the rules are too strict and old fashioned.

8. _____ Students who do not maintain a B average, are put on probation.

9. _____ A minimum of one hour of homework per class, is assigned.

10. _____ Stereos and televisions cannot be played after 7.00pm.

11. _____ Therefore, having strict rules, ensures strong discipline.

B *Divide the sentences into two groups*

A	B
Quality of Education	**Rules of the school**
_____	_____
_____	_____
_____	_____
_____	_____
_____	_____
_____	_____
_____	_____

Identifying Topic and Supporting Sentences

A   *Read the following sentences about San Francisco. Two of the sentences are **topic sentences**; two are concluding sentences, the rest are **supporting sentences**. Divide them into two groups. Some of the sentences are about the weather and some are about tourist attractions. Label the former **W** and the latter **TA**. Then write up a plan and then a paragraph for each **topic**, using the organizing charts.*

1. _____   *Therefore*, I would rather live in a cleaner city.

2. _____   Many stores are available in many shopping centres.

3. _____   A lot of big shopping arcades are available.

4. _____   Living in cities can be an *advantage*

5. _____   Both cities have congested roads with much traffic.

6. _____   *Therefore*, I would rather live in a city to enjoy the shopping

7. _____   Canals in the city back alleys are usually dirty.

8. _____   Living in these cities can be also be a *disadvantage*

9. _____   Arcades will usually provide lots of entertainment.

10. _____   Both cities have historical places to visit.

11. _____   There aren't many people who care about their rubbish disposal.

B   *Divide the sentences into two groups*

A	B
An *Advantage* Living in	**A *Disadvantage* Living in**
Big Cities	**Big Cities**
_____	_____
_____	_____
_____	_____
_____	_____
_____	_____

You are living in another city now. Write an email (50 – 70 words) to a friend (s),
telling them about your –experiences
Use the following question words to help you. *What? When?; Where?; Who; How? Do / Did you like it?*
Add *also / but* where necessary. Use **frequency adverbs** *always; sometimes* and *never*. (where needed)
Use the space below to plan your writing.

	Subject	*Verb*	*Opinion*	*Topic*
Topic Sentence (1)				
What?		**also / but**		
Who with?				
When?				
Why?				
Where?				
How?				
Concl; Do / Did you like it?				

Chapter Eight

Concluding

Sentences

Writing a *Concluding Sentence*

Use this form to help organise your paragraphs. Write a **concluding sentence** in the rectangle at the top. Write your **concluding sentence** in the final rectangle. Use these sentences to build your conclusion, adding any other words and details that you need to make it complete.

title

My Parents

My parents are very hardworking, both away from and at home.

topic sentence

My father works outside the home He is an accountant and looks after *many* clients. My mother *always* stays at home cleaning the house and preparing the meals

My father *usually* goes to work every day at 8.00am. *Sometimes* he has to visit clients at their work. He *rarely* comes home before 7.00pm, but *always* finds time to eat dinner with us.

My mother *often* gets up at 5.00am, washes all the floors and prepares breakfast for my father and my siblings. She will *then* go shopping for food and *always* prepares the evening meals.

support

support

support

Therefore,

_____

_____

_____

_____

54

Writing a *Concluding Sentence*

Use this form to help organise your paragraphs. Write a *concluding sentence* in the rectangle at the top. Write your *concluding sentence* in the final rectangle. Use these sentences to build your conclusion, adding any other words and details that you need to make it complete.

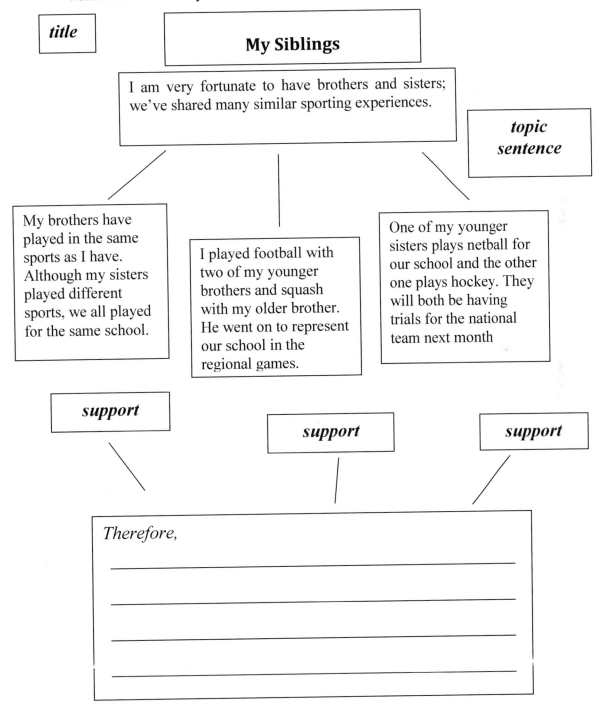

title

My Siblings

I am very fortunate to have brothers and sisters; we've shared many similar sporting experiences.

topic sentence

My brothers have played in the same sports as I have. Although my sisters played different sports, we all played for the same school.

I played football with two of my younger brothers and squash with my older brother. He went on to represent our school in the regional games.

One of my younger sisters plays netball for our school and the other one plays hockey. They will both be having trials for the national team next month

support

support

support

Therefore,

Concluding Sentences

*Complete the **concluding sentences** for each paragraph. Use the vocabulary in the body paragraphs. Pick out key words to help you (Refer to pages 37 and 58).*

Title
        My City and Kuala Lumpur

Topic Sentence 1
    Living in a city can be an *advantage*.

Supporting Sentences
    A lot of big shopping arcades are available in London and Kuala Lumpur. Also, cities provide many more places to go and visit. Regent Street and K.L.C.C. are where you can find all the big stores and you can buy many bargains in the sales. Arcades will also *usually* provide lots of entertainment. Both London and Kuala Lumpur are *often* full of historical places to visit. Such as the Tower of London and the Batu Caves. Nelson's Column and other statues reflect their history.

_____

_____

Topic Sentence 2
    But living in London and Kuala Lumpur can also be a *disadvantage*.

Supporting Sentences
    In both London and Kuala Lumpur there are more public vehicles also people don't care about their rubbish. Although London and Kuala Lumpur try to keep themselves clean, so much traffic *usually* pollute the air with their fumes. Buses and taxis as well as lorries, are the culprits. They also provide the noise that is deafening. Most large cities, like London and Kuala Lumpur, have rivers and canals that are polluted. Also the roads are not kept as clean and tidy as they should be. People are constantly throwing their rubbish out of car windows.

_____

_____

Concluding Sentences

Read the *supporting sentences* and then decide upon a suitable *title; topic sentence* and a *concluding sentence.*

A

      _____

_____

_____

First, I *often* get up late and eat breakfast. *Secondly,* I read a newspaper for a few hours. *Next,* by four-o-clock, I am *usually* hungry so I make myself a snack. *Then,* I watch TV and *sometimes* take a nap. *After that,* in the evening, I *often* go out to dinner with friends. I am *usually,* back in bed again by ten-o-clock. *Finally,* I like to relax on Sunday so that I am ready to start my week on Monday

_____

_____

B

      _____

_____

_____

First, she says *always* select the carrots that *sometimes* have their leaves still attached, they'll be fresh. *Secondly,* buy some tomatoes that are almost ripe, *never* choose squashed or bright red ones. *Next,* I want some onions, Spanish, not spring, make sure they are *always* firm. *Then,* you can select potatoes, the King Edwards type. *Finally,* at the end of the counter, buy a tin of peas, that's where they are *usually* kept.

_____

_____

C

      _____

_____

_____

First, it's a modern kitchen, nice and clean with a lot of cupboards. *Secondly,* there's a washing machine, fridge and a cooker. But there isn't a dishwasher. *Next,* there are some lovely posters on the walls, *however* there aren't any photographs. On the dining table there are some bananas and grapes

_____

_____

<u>My Mother</u>

Title

Thesis Statement	My mother *subject*	helps *verb*		me with studies and advice. *topic*
Topic Sentence 1	My mother *subject*	is *verb*	*always* *opinion*	helping me study. *topic*

Supporting Sentences

When   *When* I come home from school.

What   She helps me with my homework and tells me *what* to do if I need help.

Where   It's *usually* in our study, but she comes to the public library as well.

How   *Finally*, she directs me to the correct books and talks to me in a calm manner.

Concluding Sentence 1   *Therefore*, I can *always* rely on my mother when I am studying.

Topic Sentence 2

_____ _____ _____ _____
subject   *verb*   *opinion*   *topic*

Supporting Sentences

When   _____

What   _____

Where _____

How   _____

_____

Concluding Sentence 2   _____

_____

Now write an essay about **YOUR** sibling. Use the given *determiners,* or choose your own.

Title _____

Thesis
Statement _____ _____ _____
                       subject   *verb*   *topic*

Topic
Sentence 1 _____ _____ _____ _____
                       subject   *verb*   *opinion*   *topic*

Supporting
Sentences   *When* _____

                 What _____

                 Where _____

                 How _____

Concluding
Sentence 1 _____

Topic
Sentence 2 _____ _____ _____ _____
                       subject   *verb*   *opinion*   *topic*

Supporting
Sentences   *When* _____

                 What _____

                 Where _____

                 How _____

Concluding
Sentence 2 _____

Write about _____ and _____
Add *and / but* where necessary. Use frequency adverbs *always; sometimes* and *never*.
Use the space below to plan your writing. 120 words.

	Subject		*Verb Topic*	
*Thesis Statement*_____				
Quantifiers	**Introduction**	**Body 1** (topic)	**Body 2** (topic)	
Many	What? _____	_____	_____	
Some	When? _____	_____	_____	
Quite a few	Where? _____	_____	_____	
Not many	Who with? _____ Why? _____	_____	_____	
	How? _____	_____	_____	

Introduction

What? _____   Who with? _____

When?_____   Why? _____

Where? _____   How? _____
Body 1
What? _____

When?_____

Where? _____

Who
with? _____
Why? _____

How? _____

Conclusion_____
Body 2
What? _____

When?_____

Where? _____

Who
with? _____
Why? _____

How? _____

Conclusion _____

Write about **Supermarkets** and **Street markets**
Add *and / but* where necessary. Use *frequency adverbs* *always; sometimes* and *never*.
Use the space below to plan your writing. Use the space below to plan your writing.

	Subject	*Verb*	*Topic*
Thesis Statement **Quantifiers**	***Many* people**	use	*street and supermarkets*
	Introduction	**Body 1**	**Body 2**
		(Street markets)	*(Supermarkets)*
Many/Most — *What?*	Street/Super markets	Food/clothes *but*	Food/clothes/electrical
When?	Week-ends/days	Special days *but*	Anytime
Some *Where?*	Villages/ towns	Anywhere *but*	*Usually* towns
Quite a few *Who* with?	Singles / families	Anyone *and*	Anyone
Not many *Why?*	Buy food/clothes	Cash/barter no credit *but*	Cash/credit card can't barter
How?	Private/public trans	Car / walk *and*	Car / bus

Introduction

What? There are *many* street and supermarkets.
When? *Some* people go to street markets during mid-week or week-ends.
Where There are *always* markets everywhere.

Who *Quite a few* people frequent both.
Why? *Many* go to street markets for bargains.
Some go to supermarkets to buy on credit.
How? Access can be by private or public transport.

Body 1

What? Food and clothes can be bought in street markets, *but* clothes are not *often* bought because of the lack of changing rooms. Food is *usually* cheaper, because it's locally grown.
When? Local markets have restricted times when they are available, *but not many* are open on a daily basis.
Where? Street markets can be accessed in both villages and towns, *but* again they may only be restricted to specific days
Who With? *Some* people go to the market on their own, *and quite a lot* go to meet friends and neighbours. It is *often* a time to see old friends and for children to choose things.
Why? At street markets, people can *sometimes* have prices reduced *but* there is no opportunity to purchase anything on credit.
How? Access is *sometimes* by car, *and many* locals, walk as the market is not far from where they live.
Conclusion? Therefore, although it's easy to get to *most* street markets, it is restricted by its choice of sales.

Body 2

What? Not only can food and clothes be bought at supermarkets, *but* a wide range of electrical goods also.
When? Supermarkets are accessible every day of the week *and* stay open late.
Where? *Many* are restricted to be available only in towns *and* not many can be located in villages.
Who With? *Usually*, families frequent supermarkets *and* the latter have play areas and *many* other shops that attract the larger family groups.
Why? Supermarkets are attractive because of the opportunity for shoppers to buy things on credit, *but* even buying cash will not allow discounts to be entertained.
How? Supermarkets will be accessed by car from very rural areas *and many* are accessed by private taxis, in towns.
Conclusion? Therefore, accessibility is restricted by transport *but* the supermarkets' variety, make them popular.

Introduction   Title [   ]   <u>Getting Your Paragraph Organised</u>

[   ]

[   ]   **Thesis Statement**

Plan

Support   **Support**   **Support**

Conclusion

[   ]

My City and Kuala Lumpur

Introduction

Many cities have similar buildings. *Some* people of similar cities speak the same language. *A lot of* cities have rivers flowing through them. *Quite a few* cities have famous statues and buildings in them.

Thesis Statement

There are advantages and ***disadvantages*** to living in a city.

Plan

1. *Topic Sentence* Living in London and *Kuala Lumpur can also be a **disadvantage**.*	2. Main Sentence *Sometimes* it can be noisy, also it can be very dirty.	3. Sub-sentence Lots of traffic all day long.	4. Sub-sentence Canals and streets full of rubbish.	5. *Concl / sentence* *Therefore*, the city can be inconvenient and ***disadvantageous.***

Topic Sentence

However, living in London and Kuala Lumpur can also be a ***disadvantage***.

Support	**Support**	**Support**
In both London and Kuala Lumpur there are more public vehicles *also people don't care about their rubbish.*	Although London and Kuala Lumpur try to keep themselves clean, so much traffic *usually* pollute the air with their fumes. Buses and taxis as well as lorries are the culprits. They also provide the noise that is deafening.	*Both London and Kuala Lumpur also have rivers and canals that are heavily polluted. Also the roads are not kept as clean and tidy as they should be. People are constantly throwing their rubbish out of car windows.*

Conclusion

Therefore, I would rather live in a city that is kept much cleaner than ours.

63

My City and Kuala Lumpur

Introduction

Many cities have similar buildings. Some people of similar cities speak the same language. A lot of cities have rivers flowing through them. Quite a few cities have famous statues and buildings in them.

Thesis Statement

There are *advantages* and disadvantages to living in a city.

Plan

1. **Topic Sentence**	2. Main Sentence	3. Sub-sentence	4. Sub-sentence	5. **Concl / sentence**
Living in London and *Kuala Lumpur can be an advantage.*	*Many* places to shop. *Able to visit many places.*	Shopping for many different things is made easier.	*There are far more places to see.*	*Therefore*, the city is more convenient and *advantageous*.

Topic Sentence

Living in London and Kuala Lumpur can be an *advantage.*

Support	**Support**	**Support**
A lot of big shopping arcades are available in London and Kuala Lumpur. *Also, cities provide **many** more places to go and visit.*	Regent Street and K.L.C.C. are where you can find all the big stores and buy many bargains in the sales. Arcades will also provide lots of entertainment.	*Both London and Kuala Lumpur are **often** full of historical places to visit. Such as The Tower of London and The Batu Caves. Nelson's Column and other statues reflect their history.*

Conclusion

Therefore, I would rather live in a city to enjoy the shopping and history.

Title	<u>My City and Kuala Lumpur</u>
Introduction	*Many* cities have similar buildings. *Some* people of similar cities speak the same language. *A lot* of cities have rivers flowing through them. *Quite a few* cities have famous statues and buildings in them.
Thesis Statement	There are *advantages* and *disadvantages* to living in cities.
Topic Sentence 1	Living in a city can be an ***advantage.***
Supporting Sentences	*A lot of* big shopping arcades are available in Kuala Lumpur. Also, cities provide many more places to go and visit. Regent Street and K.L.C.C. are where you can find all the big stores and you can buy many bargains in the sales. Arcades will also *usually* provide lots of entertainment. Both London and Kuala Lumpur are *often* full of historical places to visit. Such as the Tower of London and the Batu Caves. Nelson's Column and other statues reflect their history. *Therefore, I would rather live in a city to enjoy the shopping and history.*
Topic Sentence 2	But living in London and Kuala Lumpur can also be a ***disadvantage.***
Supporting Sentences	In both London and Kuala Lumpur there are more public vehicles, also people don't care about their rubbish. Although London and Kuala Lumpur try to keep themselves clean, so much traffic *usually* pollute the air with their fumes. Buses and taxis as well as lorries, are the culprits. They also provide the noise that is deafening. Both London and Kuala Lumpur also have rivers and canals that are heavily polluted. Also the roads are not kept as clean and tidy as they should be. People are constantly throwing their rubbish out of car windows. *Therefore, I would rather live in a city that is cleaner; to enjoy the beauty it has to offer.*

My City and Kuala Lumpur

Many cities have similar buildings. *Some* people of similar cities speak the same language. *A lot of* cities have rivers flowing through them. *Quite a few* cities have famous statues and buildings in them. *There are advantages and disadvantages to living in a city.*

Living in a city can be an advantage. A lot of big shopping arcades are available in London and Kuala Lumpur. Also, cities provide *many* more places to go and visit. Regent Street and K.L.C.C. are where you can find all the big stores and you can buy *many* bargains in the sales. shopping arcades will also *usually* provide lots of entertainment. Both London and Kuala Lumpur are *often* full of historical places to visit. Such as the Tower of London and the Batu Caves. Nelson's Column and other statues reflect their history. *Therefore, I would rather live in a city to enjoy the shopping and history.*

But living in London and Kuala Lumpur can also be a disadvantage. In both London and Kuala Lumpur there are more public vehicles also people don't care about their rubbish. Although London and Kuala Lumpur try to keep themselves clean, so much traffic *usually* pollute the air with their fumes. Buses and taxis as well as lorries, are the culprits. They also provide the noise that is deafening. Both London and Kuala Lumpur also have rivers and canals that are heavily polluted. Also the roads are not kept as clean and tidy as they should be. People are constantly throwing their rubbish out of car windows. *Therefore, I would rather live in a city that is cleaner; to enjoy the beauty it has to offer.*

Chapter Nine

Concluding

Paragraphs

Title	<u>A Chosen Celebrity</u>
Introduction	Celebrities are such because they are famous. *Many* would not be called such if only *a few* people knew them. However even though they could be world-known, they might be non-entities to some people. They are *usually* recognised when they come on TV. This is because of the exposure they will receive. Actors, actresses and sportsmen will *always* be recognised, as well as singers and pop-stars.
Thesis Statement	I chose Roger Federer as my celebrity, for his tennis ability and his unassuming manner.
Topic Sentence 1	He has become the world number one tennis player since 2004.
Supporting Sentences	*First*, he became world junior champion in 1998. *Secondly* he has *always* consistently won titles. *Next*, in the 10 years to 2007, he couldn't stop winning titles. *Then*, he thrice won the Australian Open, the U.S. Open and Wimbledon in the same year. *Finally*, in 2007 the Laureaus Sports awards named him, Sportsman of the year for the third time. *Therefore*, by breaking so many records he also has a chance of surpassing Bjorn Borg's Wimbledon's record five wins.
Topic Sentence 2	Away from the tennis, Federer works to help those less fortunate than himself.
Supporting Sentences	*First*, he is *always* very sportsmanlike. He *never* argues about decisions that go against him and *usually* accepts them without a fuss. *Secondly*, he established the Roger Federer Foundation to benefit **disadvantaged** children in countries like South Africa. *Next*, he encouraged other sports stars to raise money for those devastated by the tsunami. *Then*, in 2006 he became a Goodwill Ambassador for UNICEF. *Finally*, his first UNICEF visit was to Tamil Nadu in Southern India. *Therefore*, he epitomizes everything good about a person.
Concluding Paragraph Re-phrase	
Thesis Statement Your opinions/ feelings (1) Your opinions/ feelings (2) Your opinions/ feelings (3) Your opinions/ feelings (4)	_____ _____ _____ _____ _____

	My Family and I
Title	
Introduction	The father and mother, parents, are the backbone to any family. The children, if any, also help to bond the family unit together. The father *usually* makes the decisions. Mothers will *always* maintain an orderly house. The father *rarely* cleans the house but *sometimes* might cook. The children, when able will also help share in house duties.
Thesis Statement	Families are very important in everyone's life.
Topic Sentence 1	My parents are *always* giving me advice.
Supporting Sentences	*First*, my father has *always* helped me through school and college. He is *usually* there when my homework gets too tough. *Secondly* my mother is a good cook, she *always* prepares delicious meals. *Next* she also maintains the household and it's *never* dirty. *Finally*, my father is very competent in repairing things in the house. *Therefore* both my parents have contributed to my excellent upbringing.
Topic Sentence 2	My sister and a brother have shared many good experiences.
Supporting Sentences	*First*, my brother is *younger* than me and my sister is much older. She has *always* been like a second mother to me. *Next* my brother is younger, but we *usually* like the same things. *Next* sometimes, the three of us will go out shopping together. *Finally* we *often* discuss any problems we might have. *Therefore*, I *always* manage to find time to talk to them, about anything.
Concluding Paragraph Re-phrase *Thesis Statement* Your opinions/ feelings (1) Your opinions/ feelings (2) Your opinions/ feelings (3) Your opinions/ feelings (4)	_____ _____ _____ _____ _____

Title	<u>My Parents and I</u>
Introduction	A lot of *parents* are always busy. *Parents* try and are devoted to their children. Many *parents* are at home or are working away from home. *Parents* try and share responsibilities in the home. Most *parents* are devoted to their children.
Thesis Statement	*Parents* are very important in everyone's life.
Topic Sentence 1	My father is *always* giving me advice.
Supporting Sentences	*First*, my father has *always* helped me through school and college. He is *usually* there when my homework gets too tough. He won't tell me the answers but I manage to work them out with his guidance. *Finally*, my father has reassured me regarding my future, as to what university I should attend. *Therefore*, having my father near me has meant I will *often* make the right decisions.
Topic Sentence 2	I have a hardworking mother.
Supporting Sentences	*First*, my mother is a good cook. She *always* prepares delicious meals that I like. She *usually* buys fresh vegetables, to make certain of a tasty meal. *Next* she also maintains the household and it's *never* dirty. She washes my clothes and keeps my room clean. *Finally*, she *always* finds time to talk to me. *Therefore*, having a mother like mine has helped me a lot, to understand what I must do in life.
Concluding Paragraph Re-phrase *Thesis Statement* Your opinions/ feelings (1) Your opinions/ feelings (2) Your opinions/ feelings (3) Your opinions/ feelings (4)	_____ _____ _____ _____

Title	<u>My Siblings and I</u>
Introduction	Siblings have *always* helped to keep families together. They *sometimes*, have the same shared interests. Many *often* share in household responsibilities. Siblings of the same gender, quite *often* become close friends.
Thesis Statement	*Siblings* are very important in family life.
Topic Sentence 1	My brother is *always* playing games that I like.
Supporting Sentences	*First*, although we don't like the same teams, we *always* watch football matches together. My team beat his team last week, but we *never* quarreled about it. I can *always* ask my brother for advice about anything. *Therefore*, we will *usually* be able to work out any problems we have.
Topic Sentence 2	I am also fortunate to have sisters.
Supporting Sentences	*First*, one has been like a second mother to me. She is *always* there to give me advice. My other sister is slightly *younger* than me. Although I don't share the same things as my brother, we still have similar interests. The three of us will *often* go shopping together at week-ends. *Therefore*, we all have a bond between us.
Concluding Paragraph Re-phrase *Thesis Statement* Your opinions/ feelings (1) Your opinions/ feelings (2) Your opinions/ feelings (3) Your opinions/ feelings (4)	_____ _____ _____ _____ _____

My Father

<table>
<tr>
<td>Introduction</td>
<td>Fathers, are the backbone to any family. The father usually makes the decisions. A father rarely cleans the house but sometimes might cook. Fathers generally provide the family income.</td>
</tr>
<tr>
<td>Thesis Statement</td>
<td>In this essay I will discuss the **advantages** and **disadvantages** of being a father.</td>
</tr>
<tr>
<td>Topic Sentence 1</td>
<td>My father has been supportive, always gave me advice and has helped me through my growing years.</td>
</tr>
<tr>
<td>Supporting Sentences</td>
<td>First, my father has always helped me through school and college. He usually took me to my primary school when I first started going to school. Secondly my father has watched me when I played football or rugby. Then my father is very understanding if I didn't come home on time and would explain the dangers involved. Finally, before I reached my teens he would explain some of the fine points of my adolescence.</td>
</tr>
<tr>
<td>Concluding Sentence</td>
<td>Therefore my father has contributed to an excellent start to my upbringing.</td>
</tr>
<tr>
<td>Topic Sentence 2</td>
<td>In addition I am very fortunate to have a father that understands teenage hood.</td>
</tr>
<tr>
<td>Supporting Sentences</td>
<td>First, just before I went to college, my father helped me through my O-levels and A-levels. He gave me the confidence to achieve high grades. Secondly, these helped me choose the college I wanted to go to. Next, my transitions were made less complicated because of my father's patience. Finally, I always manage to find time to talk to him, about anything.</td>
</tr>
<tr>
<td>Concluding Sentence</td>
<td>Therefore, having a father throughout one's teenage life can be of great benefit, in understanding problems that you could encounter.</td>
</tr>
<tr>
<td>Topic Sentence 3</td>
<td>However, a friend of mine is very unfortunate to have a father that doesn't understand teenage hood.</td>
</tr>
<tr>
<td>Supporting Sentences</td>
<td>First, just before he went to college, his father didn't help him. He didn't give him the confidence to achieve high grades. Secondly, these didn't help him choose the college he wanted to go to. Next, his transitions were made more complicated because of his father's lack of patience. Finally, he didn't always manage to find time to talk to him, about anything.</td>
</tr>
<tr>
<td>Concluding Sentence</td>
<td>Not having a father throughout one's teenage life, can be a great discomfort, in understanding problems that you could encounter.</td>
</tr>
<tr>
<td>Concluding Paragraph</td>
<td>Therefore the bond between us is could be often very strong. Or it could be weak, if we respect each other's roles in the family. This will always help to maintain stability. It will also give us good ideas. This could be emulated in one's own family.</td>
</tr>
</table>

(390words)

(Note: These are five paragraphs. They're separated to emphasise distinctions).

Chapter Ten

Exercises

Topic Sentence Construction

A.   Below is a *topic sentence*. Write good *supporting sentences* in the spaces provided. Make sure when you plan, you also.....

- begin with a *title*.
- contain five or more sentences that support the *topic sentence*.
- end with *concluding sentence*.
- use correct *capitalisation; punctuation* and *word order*.
- Use *frequency adverbs*.

The first day of school is always hectic because of the registration of new classes.

B.   Read the paragraph below and then decide on a *suitable title; topic sentence* and *concluding sentence*.

_____

_____

First, I *always* pack the things I need for the hike: the stove; cooking utensils and the tent. I may add a few tins of fruit and cartons of drinks. *Next*, I put a few clothes together, remembering to pack my swimming trunks. I *often* find a stream to swim in. *After that*, I collect my cheque and money. *Finally*, I get dressed in my hiking gear.

_____

_____

Daniel's Birthday Party

washing-up	sister	dancing	uncle
stereo	father	kitchen	mother
aunt	guitar	friends	drinking
taking pictures	coloured balloons	birthday cake	grand mother

Write a paragraph about Daniel's party. Use the words above to help you. Remember to also use, *capital letters* and the *correct punctuation*. You should include a *topic sentence; supporting sentences* and a *concluding sentence*. Where possible also include: *signal words* and *frequency adverbs*.

_____

_____

_____

_____

_____

_____

_____

_____

_____

_____

_____

_____

_____

_____

You are living in another country now. Write an email (60 – 75 words) to a friend, **telling them about your *Weekly Routine*.**
Use the question words, below, to help you. Add *also / but* where necessary.
Use frequency adverbs *always; sometimes* and *never*, (where needed).
Use the space below to plan your writing.

Title _____

Intro _____
(Topic sentence
Support Sentences
What? _____ *Why*? _____
  (subject)   (reason/s)
When? _____ *Where*? _____
  (time)   (location)
Who with? _____ *How*? _____
  (person/s)   (method)

      Do/Did _____
      you like it,

_____

_____

_____

_____

_____

_____

_____

_____

_____

_____

Satellite and Internet Television

Many people have strong feelings about the value of television, especially now that programs are available through the satellite over the Internet. There are people who suggest that increased access to these programs does more harm than good. However, there are also some who insist that it is a good thing.

*Complete the supporting sentences for the two body paragraphs and concluding paragraphs. Remember to include **frequency adverbs** where possible*

Satellite and Internet TV does a lot of harm. _____

_____

_____

_____

_____

_____

_____

However, some say that they are both a good thing._____

_____

_____

_____

_____

_____

_____

_____

Therefore,_____

_____

_____

_____

Write about _____ and _____

Add *and / but* where necessary. Use frequency adverbs *always; sometimes* and *never*. Use the space below to plan your writing. Write **three** paragraphs (about 150 – 175 words). Remember to include *topic; supporting* and *concluding sentences*. Also *signal words* where necessary.

	Subject	_Verb_	_Topic_
Thesis Statement _____			

Quantifiers		**Introduction**	**Body 1** (topic)	**Body 2** (topic)
Many	*What?*	_____	_____	_____
Some	*When?*	_____	_____	_____
Quite a few	*Where?*	_____	_____	_____
	Who with?	_____	_____	_____
Not many	*Why?*	_____	_____	_____
	How?	_____	_____	_____

_____

_____

_____

_____

_____

_____

_____

_____

_____

_____

_____

Summary

I hope that this book has enlightened you to the practical ways of *writing essays*. I want to point out a few things when writing the *body* and *concluding paragraphs*.

1. When deciding on the *topics*, for the *paragraphs*, it is important to decide if they concur when linking them (see page 49).

2. If the *linking words* are similar but the *topics* differ, you may want to use *one body paragraph* and a *concluding sentence* for both topics, (see page 54). Here there are many connotations to the topics. But the overriding decision maker could come in *a two or three sentence concluding paragraph,* (see page 54).

3. However, if there is a conflict in the *topics*, then two body paragraphs must be used to emphasise the differences, (see page 56 to 66). Here the emphasis is on how very strong the argument is on the differences. The concluding paragraph may also leave readers to make up their own minds and introduce other ideas (pages 68 to 72).

Either way, I trust you will find enormous pleasure in putting your own ideas across, with the help of this book.

HAPPY WRITING

Phil Rashid

INDEX

Bibliography

English for Malaysians
J.S Solomon' Chuah Ai Bee and Susila S Solomon
Pelanduk Publications

Ready to Write
A First Composition Text
Second Edition
Karen Blanchard & Christine Root

English Language Workbook
Early Learner Publications Sdn. Bhd

How to Write an Essay. Original full-length version

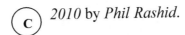 *2010* by *Phil Rashid*.

Edited by: Dr Yahaya Abdullah, Siti Hajar Husna

NOTES